A souvenir guide

Lindisfarne Castle
Northumberland

Victoria Gibson

GW00399903

National Trust

This page Lindisfarne Castle in the distance

Opposite This text is extracted from a diary entry by Oswald Falk, one of the Castle's later owners and residents (see page 10)

March 1930

'My guests have gone and I am alone in the Castle tonight, a night in early June. It is nine o'clock and I go out on to the lower battery to talk with Jack about the day's doings and the plans for the next day. It has been a cloudless day, as still as any can be on the Island, and Jack thinks the weather will hold.

There is a slight swell of the sea which barely has the strength to break when it reaches the shore. We can hear it lapping on the rocks below. There is no stir amongst the flowers growing in the niches of the battery walls, wallflowers, thrift, and harebells chiefly. Even the harebells are still.

The sun is near setting over the Cheviots, and the green of the grass round the Castle is becoming vivid. Sea birds are calling and Jack points them out to me, sitting on the Rigg a quarter of a mile away, a heron stands in a pool, motionless as a bronze sculpture. It is cold now, and I go in to the Ship Room where there is always a log fire winter and summer alike.

Jack piles on some fresh logs, and we light the candles of the large candelabra, some twenty or more, for the windows of the Ship room are small and it is never very light there even at midday. A little more gossip and then Jack goes off to bed, for he will get up very early for the fishing. He closes the door and I am left alone, a bottle of port by my side, the ticking of the clock and a little crackling from the fire the only sound … The fire burns with a blue flame for the logs of ship's timber have salt in them.

I go up the little steps to the small high windows to look down from them on to the meadow some sixty feet below. It surrounds the castle rock on the island side. There the long horned highland cattle are still grazing, and I can hear their tearing of the grass. There is an occasional clash from their interlocking horns.

I go back to the fire side and port and Florio's Montaigne – It is getting dark and I put on some gramophone records, Chopin in melancholy mood, and Chaliapin in Boris Godunov. More port and more Chaliapin, a little drunk with sensation – the silent intervals become ghostly and frightening. Is it me?

… More port and more music exclusively Russian now. Then silence again, but I can't read, and at last I light my hooded candle and go up the winding stone stairs to my bed.'

Oswald Falk

A Rural Retreat

In 1901, *Country Life* founder Edward Hudson took one look at the ruined fort perched on top of Beblowe Crag and knew it was special.

'I have taken a fancy to the place and know I should like it; I am keen on the sea, and restoring a place like this properly, would fall in with my hobbies. I want to make a little dock for a small yacht, and I should like to be allowed to make some rough links on the Island; all this however I could settle with Mr Crossman when we meet.'

Edward Hudson, writing to George Bolam
to convince him he would be a good tenant, December 1901

All about Edward

After a stint in a solicitor's office as a teen, 21-year-old Edward Hudson (1854–1936) joined his father's successful printing firm. Twenty-two years later, aged 43, he founded Country Life Magazine Ltd., becoming chairman and editor. *Country Life* was an early lifestyle magazine and went from strength-to-strength after its founding. To this day, every issue includes an article on a country house.

After one failed engagement (see page 8), Hudson married aged 74; his new wife was the editor of *Homes and Gardens* magazine, Ellen Woolrich.

Left A photograph of Hudson, date unknown

Above Hudson with his live-in handyman, Jack Lilburn (see pages 16–17 for more on Jack and his family)

The island's coastguards had left the fort uninhabited. However its outer walls were strong (though functional, rather than ornamental) and the inner buildings were neglected, but standing. An intelligent, determined man with a big heart, Hudson saw the potential.

In December 1901, Hudson contacted the land agent for Lindisfarne, George Bolam. By early 1902, he had leased the Castle from the Crossman Estates (who in turn had leased the Castle from the crown). By mid-1902, Lindisfarne was his.

> 'I want to amuse myself with the place.'
> Hudson, writing to Bolam, 26 March 1902

Sir Edwin Lutyens (1869–1944)

Although it was Hudson who bought Lindisfarne, the mark of his companion Edwin Lutyens is equally – if not more – prominent in the Castle today.

Lutyens was the leading architect of his day. Due to illness, he didn't attend public school or university, but his future career became clear early on. He enrolled in Kensington School of Art, London in 1885, but left prematurely, after just two years, feeling he had no more to learn there. Just a year later he set up his own practice. He later became the first architect to be awarded the Order of Merit.

In 1887, Lutyens married Emily Lytton. They went on to have five children: Barbra (Barbie), Robert, Ursula, Elisabeth and Mary. But letters written throughout Lutyens' time at Lindisfarne suggest their marriage was not a happy one.

The fun-loving architect

Ned, as he was affectionately known, was quirky, eccentric and childish. Those in his company loved his wit and sense of humour, even though he was socially awkward. 'Never since the days of Sheridan and Goldsmith has a man of genius been so widely beloved,' wrote Harold Nicholson after Lutyens' death. 'He adopted an identical attitude of bubbling friendliness whether he was talking to a Queen Dowager or a cigarette girl, a Cardinel or a school boy' (*Friday Mornings*, 1944). Lutyens was said to be particularly good with his clients and 'got the best out of the workmen … for he had a deep respect for their craftsmanship as well as a knowledge and understanding of it' (Mary Lutyens, The Lutyens Trust, 1981).

Above Lutyens at his desk c.1926, photographed by Edward Gooch

Left Lutyens sketched this at Lindisfarne. It depicts him, his daughter Barbie, and Hudson going to bed at the Castle

From fort to holiday home

Known for his funny sketches and carrying around a blackboard on his belt just in case he needed to jot something down, Lutyens' personality made Lindisfarne Castle what it is today.

'He has offered for a castle! …
Too funny.'

> Lutyens, writing about Hudson to his wife,
> Emily, 12 August 1901

When Hudson exclaimed 'Got Lindisfarne!', Lutyens needed no more words. The challenge was to fit a modern holiday home within the neglected fort's Tudor ramparts.

Hudson envisioned Lindisfarne Castle being a place for relaxation, enjoyment and to create memories. Even before restoration had started, 'Huddy' (as Lutyens called him) was planning a 'picnic' for 30 guests over Christmas – something Lutyens thought was a great idea.

The Lutyens effect

Lutyens started work in 1902, creating an L-shaped house, successfully integrating the fort's old east and west buildings and removing the battlements, resulting in a softer silhouette.

Building work began in May 1903 and the first phase was completed in July 1906. The Long Gallery bedrooms (see pages 22–25) were added in a second 'phase' of changes in 1912.

Above **The exterior of Lindisfarne in 1906**

Opposite above **The Castle's entrance in 1913, seen from across the Lower Battery to the east**

Lutyens' fondness for mixing building materials, including stone, brick, slate and cobbles, is clear to see. Hidden staircases, maze-like passages, precise designs and stylish finishing touches within Lindisfarne Castle are all clearly Lutyens.

However the architect's love affair with the building's history meant that no electricity or gas was installed.

Lutyens after Lindisfarne

Lindisfarne was Lutyens' first castle. About the same time he took on two more. Lambay Castle off the coast of Dublin was next (1905) and then Castle Drogo in Devon (1910–30) – the latter is now also looked after by the National Trust. Each is very different, but both show Lutyens' understanding of the medieval architecture.

Hudson was an early patron of Lutyens, his favourite architect and life-long friend. He owned two other Lutyens-designed houses, Deanery Gardens in Sonning, Berkshire (c.1899–1907), and Plumpton Place, Sussex (1928–36), and when the *Country Life* offices needed expanding, it was Lutyens who designed the new headquarters in Covent Garden.

After the renovation

Even though Hudson bought the Castle outright in 1918, it became quite a trip from London and was expensive to maintain. A letter dated 6 June 1910 reveals Hudson had undertaken renovations on the Castle estimated at £5–6,000 (the equivalent of about £50–65,000 today) and initially planned to do more. Later, he commented on how it had been 'a far more expensive venture than he could have ever imagined' and, in 1920, he put his beloved holiday home up for sale.

'I am very keen on the place, it is so interesting and amusing.'

Hudson, writing to George Bolam,
November 1903

The Arts and Crafts Movement
Lutyens was a well-known practitioner of the Arts and Crafts Movement, something clearly visible throughout Lindisfarne. The influential movement flourished in Europe and North America in the late 19th and early 20th centuries and stood for traditional craftsmanship using simple forms, advocated economic and social reform and has been said to have been anti-industrial. Other well-known Arts and Crafts Movement figures include architect Augustus Pugin, writer John Ruskin and designer and poet William Morris.

Love and hate: Hudson's guests

Under Hudson's care, Lindisfarne Castle welcomed a wealth of people: the flamboyant, the talented, the brave and even the royal.

Above Golfers and their caddies playing on the James Braid-designed golf course, 1910

Below Madame Suggia, photographed with Hudson at Lindisfarne c.1919

Hudson was a man of few words, but clearly enjoyed entertaining. When he was at Lindisfarne, he threw dinner parties for his accomplished guests one week and filled the halls with Lutyens' children's laughter the next. A stone's throw from the coast, the Castle was ideal for fishing, donkey rides on the beach and golf (a nine-hole course was designed by five times Open Championship winner James Braid, at Hudson's request).

Many loved the Castle's unusual position and praised the architecture. Others loathed it. Either way, Lindisfarne was a stage for romance and tragedy.

The lady of the castle: Madame Guilhermina Suggia (1885–1950)

The internationally renowned cellist Madame Guilhermina Suggia was born in Oporto, Portugal and had been a student of pre-eminent cellist Pablo Casals, in Paris, before moving to England in 1914.

Madame Suggia was a frequent visitor to the Castle, and on 12 March 1919 her engagement to Hudson was announced in *The Times*. But they never married. There's no known reason as to why the engagement was called off. Considering the era, with Hudson's wealth and her blossoming career, perhaps Suggia chose to avoid marriage rather than become a 'housewife'. They remained friends, however.

The writer: Giles Lytton Strachey (1880–1932)

One man who was not a fan of Lindisfarne Castle – or its host – from the get-go was Lytton Strachey, author of *Eminent Victorians,* co-founder of the Bloomsbury Group and biographer. In August 1918, he wrote: 'Hudson you know – a pathetically dreary figure – so curiously repulsive, too … and so, somehow, lost. He seemed a fish, gliding underwater, and star-struck – looking up with adoring eyes through his own dreadful element to Suggia in her inaccessible heaven.

'His castle seemed to me a poor affair – except for the situation, which is magnificent, and the great foundation and massive battlements, whence one has amazing prospects of sea, hills, other castles, etc – extraordinarily romantic – on every side.

'But the building itself is all timid Lutyens – very dark, with nowhere to sit, and nothing but stone under, over, & round you, which produces a distressing effect – especially when one's hurrying downstairs late for dinner – to slip would be instant death. No – not a comfortable place, by any means.'

The poet: Siegfried Loraine Sassoon (1886–1967)

Sassoon was a soldier and renowned First World War poet. He was wounded fighting in France and discharged from the army. Troubled and lonely, his experiences with treatment for shell shock during the time of his visit made the trip even more poignant. He described listening to Suggia play as 'an experience which I will always remember with gratitude. It seemed as though I had arrived at the end of a pilgrimage, to find peace and absolution in an hour of incomparable music. For it was the first time I felt completely remote and absolved from the deadly constraints of war.'

The soldier: Billy Congreve (1891–1916)

Billy Congreve, whose parents were friends of Hudson, stayed at the Castle in 1909 to recover from diphtheria. Hudson grew very fond of Billy during the boy's convalescence and was seriously considering leaving the Castle to him in his will. But this was not to be: following his recovery, Billy served in France during the First World War, winning medals for bravery. However, in July 1916 – only a month after he married – he was killed in action while tending to wounded comrades on the Somme. He was posthumously awarded the Victoria Cross for his actions; he and his father are one of only three father/son duos to both have received the award.

Above Billy Congreve in army uniform. His only daughter was born eight months after he died

Below left Visitors return to the mainland after visiting the island in 1910

Later residents and royals

After Hudson, two more owners enjoyed Lindisfarne Castle before it was bequeathed to the National Trust in 1944.

The stockbroker: Oswald Toynbee Falk (1879–1972)

On 17 April 1920, an advertisement for Lindisfarne Castle appeared that read: 'to be sold, free-hold … with planning for more rooms and its very important collection of antique furniture'. The stockbroker and economist Oswald Falk bought it the following year.

At a young age, Falk developed a reputation for intellectual brilliance combined with an 'explosive personality' (close friend Nicholas Davenport, *Memoirs of a City Radical,* 1974). He rarely hid his temper and may have acted brashly in his decisions but this brought results; consequently he gained friends for this, as well as respect, in London.

Falk sold the Castle in around 1928.

The banker: Sir Edward Adolphe Sinauer de Stein (1887–1965)

Eton-educated de Stein served in the King's Royal Rifle Corps throughout the First World War. He escaped unscathed and with the rank of Major. From Major to merchant banker, de Stein's talent lay in assessing companies and predicting their success. De Stein was a keen sportsman, fisherman and an amateur landscape gardener, so it's no surprise that he bought Lindisfarne Castle when Falk put it up for sale.

But in 1944, after 15 years of family life at Lindisfarne, de Stein presented the Castle to the National Trust. He also bequeathed many furnishings original to Hudson's aesthetic, as well as his own introductions and others by Falk. His only condition was that the lease went to his younger sister, Gladys. This remained so until her death in 1968.

Royal visits

Lindisfarne has welcomed a number of stately guests over the years.

In November 1679, James II, Duke of York at the time, visited Holy Island en route to the Scottish Parliament.

Above The April 1920 advert that prompted Falk to buy the freehold to Lindisfarne Castle

Opposite above The Prince and Princess of Wales' visit in July 1908, depicted outside Lindisfarne Priory

Opposite below HRH Charles, Prince of Wales, outside the Castle during his visit in 2012

The Prince and Princess of Wales (the future George V and Queen Mary) came to the Castle on 2 July 1908, during Lutyens' renovations. Lutyens was more than happy to joke with the Prince about the drains. A detailed letter written by Lutyens to his wife is the best record of the day. While a nervous Hudson played host, Lutyens waited at the portcullis door and, as the Prince walked up to the Castle, he overheard an aide explaining how the 'place has been rebuilt by E. Lutyens', at which point Lutyens, in typical fashion, shouted, 'High [sic], Stop. I'm here'.

The Prince was alarmed by the ramp to the Castle, which was without any sort of wall to prevent people falling, and became anxious to leave when he found the tide was rising. Considering that the future King George V was a sailor by training, Lutyens found him 'over nervous' where the tides were concerned.

When Queen Elizabeth II came in 1958, Sir Edward de Stein entertained her at lunch while the Duke of Edinburgh went off to play polo. In 2012, her son and heir Charles, Prince of Wales also paid a visit.

'When I told him how I had proposed to drain the Castle with a gun etc. he said, "oh yes, drains, of course, drains" without a smile.'

Lutyens, describing the Prince and Princess of Wales' visit in 1908

Today, a trip to this 'dainty little fort' (Chetham Society, 1844) provides an insight into how it might have felt to be a guest of Edward Hudson.

But first you have to get there: access to Lindisfarne Castle's only outer door is up a shallow stone ramp scaling the southern side of Beblowe Crag.

The boat sheds

In the north east of England, fishermen traditionally used redundant herring boats as storage sheds. These have disappeared over the years, but Holy Island is one of the few places they can still be seen. There are still several around the island's harbour, and the three next to the Castle are owned by the National Trust.

Lutyens installed two in 1906, and a third was added in 1912. Sadly these were destroyed by arson in 2005. Stuck on the mainland, a fire engine couldn't reach the sheds until the tide to the island had gone out; two of the three sheds were burnt beyond repair and the third was badly damaged. The following year, the two ruined sheds were replaced using a 19th-century herring keelboat that was due to be disposed of. The Trust renovated the third. They currently serve as storage sheds and also house lockers for visitors and a small member-recruitment office.

The Lower Battery

This area was intended to be used for defence. By 1683, there would have been as many as 12 guns in fixed positions looking out between the crenellations. Lutyens left the two, now empty, gun emplacements, which were added in the 1880s for the Volunteer Coast Artillery, as he wanted to nurture the building's history and blend the old with the new. In more recent years, caretaker George Lilburn had a pigeon loft here.

From this Battery, you can see the nearby Farne Islands, famous for their puffins and seals. Hudson took advantage of his Castle's position and planned trips to them for many of his guests – no fewer than seven excursions took place between 20 June and 4 July 1912.

The Lutyens Effect

Lutyens replaced the Victorian sash windows with new, mullioned ones with leaded lights and even added the whinstone arches above them (the whinstone arches can be seen in the photo on page 7 – they are relieving arches, made of whin. Mullioned windows are those divided vertically, perhaps by stone or wood). He rebuilt most of this elevation, including constructing the large tower on the left above the door, while managing to retain the original stonework. He also partly rebuilt the block of buildings at the western side of the Battery to include a hall and kitchen with bedrooms above.

The walkway includes a herringbone pattern: this is one of Edwin Lutyens' favourite designs and there's plenty more of it both outside and in.

Eyes and ears and …

Towards the door is a small building. Prior to Lutyens' restoration, it had been an outdoor toilet with a flat roof. For Hudson it was a larder with a new pantile roof or 'top hat'. On the outside of the Castle there's a drain-pipe, seeming to act as a 'nose'. It's thought that this is one of many faces integrated into the Castle by the fun-loving Lutyens.

Writer's retreat

This photograph shows Strachey's visit to Lindisfarne in 1918 (see page 8). Among the other guests pictured is his publisher, William Heinemann (fifth from left). Hudson invited Strachey (third from left) because he wanted him to write for *Country Life*. We're not sure why Heinemann accompanied his author on the trip – was it to visit his alleged friend, Hudson, or to ward his author off the project?

Opposite Upturned boats used as fishermen's huts remain scattered across Holy Island

Above Bringing a fisherman's hut to the Castle in 1912

The Entrance Hall

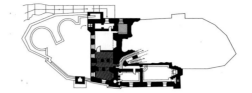

This area was originally three separate spaces. Before Lutyens remodelled the interior, visitors were met by a long corridor which ran through the centre and just left of where the Ship Room fireplace is now.

This gave the garrison the straightest and quickest route from the ammunition and powder stores to the Lower Battery. On the right, a guard-room (or officers' kitchen) would have been by the fireplace. To the left was a door leading to the kitchen, including a staircase to the quarters above.

The Lutyens effect

Lutyens took great inspiration from Durham Cathedral and this area demonstrates that perfectly. The original partition walls were replaced with grand, imposing columns with curved bases which echo the nave of Durham Cathedral (although even though it might appear otherwise, the ones at Lindisfarne rest on the slate floor, not pedestals). In the doorway, perfectly rounded bricks form an empty portcullis groove.

A new chimneypiece was installed and the old staircase, near the westernmost column which once ascended to the officers' quarters, was removed. The stones of the arches spanning the room were left partially uncovered, suggesting other such 'medieval' masonry lurks beneath.

The Wind Indicator

Notable artist and cartographer MacDonald Gill was commissioned to fill the space here with a painted mural and wind indicator. Along with a Mr Grissell, he carried out the work over the winter of 1912.

The main painting shows a fictitious engagement with the Spanish Armada. The castles on the coast and Lindisfarne are all depicted as they were in 1588. St Cuthbert is on the island while monks are shown in the long-dissolved priory.

Curious as to how the Wind Indicator worked? The mechanism, mainly the link between the drive shafts leading to the Hall (left) and the roof (right), passes under a section of the East Bedroom floor (see pages 26–27) and up to the roof behind the large armoire. Visitors standing in that room may hear it moving.

The Snewke or Coiny warren

THE GERMAN SEA

Cotes crosse

HOLY ILANDE LINDISFARNE

The Abbey

The Castle

The Haven

Shelruk Poole

Mannel head

THE INVINCIBLE ARMADA

'We've got to make those commuters laugh!'
In 1914, MacDonald Gill was also responsible for helping save the London Underground. Back then the service was far from efficient or pleasant to use, so its newly-appointed commercial director, Frank Pick, attempted to rebrand it. As well as commissioning the now-famous font, he asked MacDonald Gill to produce a poster that would make Londoners feel proud of their journey, want to visit the city's attractions – and laugh.

The result was the 'Wonderground Map'. Hung at every station, this eye-catching poster, described by the BBC in 2014 as a 'mixture of fantasy and topological accuracy', was an 'instant hit with the travelling public' and paved the way for more posters and art on the Tube, a tradition that continues today.

MacDonald Gill also worked for the Empire Marketing Board, and, in 1940, designed a 'Tea Revives the World' poster. Hugely popular at the time, this remains on sale in many poster shops.

Above The ornate MacDonald Gill-designed Wind Indicator

Opposite Lutyens-designed archways in the Entrance Hall

The Kitchen and Scullery

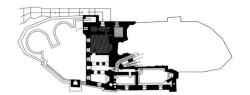

When Hudson acquired the Castle, he recruited islanders Jack Lilburn ('Wheeler' to locals), a retired fisherman, and his wife Hannah, who moved in. Jack was most likely quite happy with their new living arrangement since it would have been easy compared to his fishing days. The Kitchen and adjacent Scullery became the family's domain.

Jack and Hannah's children, George and Linda, and their children, continued three generations of caretakers at Lindisfarne Castle: the family worked here until 1968, leaving when the National Trust took over.

Cooking, cleaning and carrying
Hannah prepared meals for Hudson's grand gatherings in this room: guests enjoyed sirloin, fowl, legs of mutton and even lobsters. In the 1930s, Linda and her sister-in-law Jean prepared recipes such as milk jelly, boiled rabbit, 'Snowman Cake' and 'Guy Fawkes Pudding' (probably parkin).

Hannah was also responsible for Castle housework. Jack did maintenance, undertook odd jobs such as fetching coal or firewood, and delivered Hudson's guests to the Castle by horse and cart, and boat. If the tide was in, he physically carried them through the shallow waters.

The Lutyens effect
First referred to as a Kitchen in a Board of Ordnance ground plan of 1742, this was originally a much larger room than the one here today. Images taken during Hudson's time show that numerous changes were made to the Kitchen and surrounds. In one, the photographer is standing in an area that is now the Entrance Hall. The other shows Barbie Lutyens with the wall behind her intact, where a doorway is now.

The court cupboard and unusual cupboard at the back of the settle, which was used for hanging bacon, were acquired for the Castle. Lutyens also added the range and a new chimneypiece in 1906.

Southerly winds often blow through the Scullery from the portcullis slot. The positioning of the bacon settle was probably no coincidence as it shelters the area around the range.

Lutyens had the oak table and long dresser designed specifically for this room and they were introduced after the building work. It could be speculated that the dresser was designed with the larger room in mind, which might explain why it feels a little imposing in this smaller space.

'There is no master and servant business between us, we are just two friends – very fine friends – and I am very much moved by the love and friendship you and your wife give me.'

Hudson, writing to Jack Lilburn in December 1921, explaining that he had sold the Castle

Below Jack and Hannah Lilburn pictured in the Kitchen by the bacon settle, c.1920

Opposite A view of the Kitchen today

The Scullery

Tucked away opposite the north wall is a door leading into the Scullery. Previously a basic store area, it is identified as 'Room no. 2, 1 Man' in an 1883 plan, suggesting it was once accommodation during an emergency.

The Lutyens effect

This small room houses a sink, storage cupboard and a boiler for heating. It's uncertain when the boiler was installed, but a recently discovered date stamp reads 1956. It once heated the Castle, but was last used around 1970. After that the Castle was electrified and night-storage heaters were installed.

Being directly above the first door into the Castle, you may not be surprised to find a large winding mechanism with three steel cords, used to operate the portcullis at the main door. But what is less expected is that the portcullis was not included in the original 16th-century fort – Lutyens added it as a feature. It is really a decorative addition, typical of Lutyens' romantic approach to the Castle's history, and makes the building appear older than it actually is.

Caring for the Lilburns

This area provided accommodation for Hannah Lilburn when she was ill. In one instance Hudson – known for looking after his staff – ensured a doctor came to visit her once a day for eight weeks.

The Dining Room

The perfect space for Hudson to entertain, this room was the setting for his grand dinner parties. Guests would be served lobster or steak and showered with champagne. Madame Suggia, J. M. Barrie (author of *Peter Pan)* and Siegfried Sassoon would all have eaten here, looked after by the Lilburns.

However some guests may have become a little over-enthusiastic: during his visit in September 1918, Lytton Strachey described one as having 'a voice like a megaphone', and making a very long, 'heartfelt' speech to Hudson's health.

The Lutyens effect

Lutyens probably made very few changes to this room – but his touch can still be seen. Although the low vertical walls on the north and south sides date from the 1570s, a 1683 plan shows that the Dining Room door was once at the eastern end of the passageway. Its move was one of Lutyens' alterations, revealed by his signature pink stone visible on either side of the wall.

The blues
The blue wall at the western end is regularly monitored by the National Trust and occasionally requires retouching by a specialist conservator. The wall itself is not covered by a single shade of blue, so several need to be matched to ensure a sympathetic restoration.

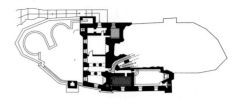

He also apparently opted for the brazen blue wall (though the present-day version was restored in the 1970s), had the chimneypiece rebuilt and the familiar herringbone brickwork floor laid. Small but effective details include the medieval inglenook seats in the fireplace, a common feature of the Arts and Crafts Movement (see page 7).

The tracery window containing a tiny piece of 17th-century Flemish stained glass was incorporated. To ensure the neo-Gothic reference was not hidden, the curtains hang on special rods that swing out against the side walls.

The dining table

Lutyens designed the large dining table specifically for this room. Such was his attention to detail that the underside of the table-top was sanded down to prevent it from snagging on guests' clothing.

The old and the new

Of the three hugely prominent features within this room, two were installed before Lutyens arrived. Only the blue wall was – we think – his work.

The vaulted ceiling was installed during the 18th century, when the room was used by the garrison as an officers' kitchen and perhaps a shell-filling room. The Queen's Battery was directly above so it had to withhold the weight of the guns.

Another eye-catching element – and evidence of the room's earliest use – is the bread-oven situated on the eastern side of the room. It's extremely uncommon to see one this old with a complete dome.

Some less prominent, but equally interesting, features are the curious markings to the left of the doorway. Some are stonemasons' 'stamps'; however, the initials are unusual. The precise date of these is unknown and because the room has changed since its first build and the entrance would have been vertical, the stone could quite possibly originally have been located elsewhere in the Castle.

Left A view of the Dining Room, including the blue wall that, we think, was painted by Lutyens

Right Linda Lilburn working in the Dining Room

The Ship Room

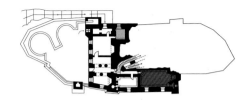

One of the largest rooms in the Castle, the Ship Room was used by Hudson as a drawing room. Here his guests listened to concerts by Madame Suggia while islanders and fishermen gathered under the windows to hear her play.

'It's my one memory of Mother picking me up and putting me on the window sill so that I could see this lovely lady in this magnificent gown.'

Lindisfarne local and family friend of the Lilburns, Elfreda Elford, describes Madame Suggia

Hudson's younger visitors might have enjoyed a very different sort of entertainment: 'We had a fire screen … the bottom part of which could be moved up leaving a gap at the bottom', remembered one of Lutyens' daughters, Mary. 'It was perfect for playing French Revolutions, and Hudson was most obliging in kneeling on the floor and putting his head through the gap so we

could guillotine him.' Although this particular incident may have actually taken place at Hudson's London home, it gives an insight into how the normally-shy Hudson might have amused children when they visited Lindisfarne.

Patches of the past

The eastern wall, to the right as you walk into the Ship Room, was originally green – as seen in this image taken in 2008. In December 2008 the plasterwork – and green paint – was carefully removed for conservation purposes. The National Trust building team removed the entire contents of the room to the Dining Room with only the chart table and dower chest remaining carefully protected. There are still small patches of green visible on the wall, especially on the hinge holding up the ship.

Left The room's eponymous model ship

This page A view of the Ship Room; the model ship can be seen hanging above the table

The Lutyens effect

The look of the room today is based on an image taken c.1912. Many of the items are the ones Hudson had on display in the room, most notably the model ship hanging from the barrel vault and coffee-warmer.

It is the model ship after which the room is apparently named. It is a replica of the *Henrietta of Amsterdam,* an 1840s merchant ship. Lutyens had Dutch seafaring ancestors who may have inspired this addition.

The room was originally used as three separate storerooms. Lutyens not only removed them, but extended the room westwards to install the grand fireplace. A dividing line can be seen in the ceiling where the extension was made. Unfortunately the fire itself wasn't quite as practical as it was impressive, often filling the room with smoke when in use.

The floor bricks – laid out in a precise pattern – were originally used as ballast in merchant shipping, and so will probably have been available in large numbers.

The simple Dutch Rococo china-cabinet is painted with a scene of peasant life on the lower doors and hanging just above the fireplace is a carved-wood achievement of arms of George I. There is an English-oak gate-leg table and a Flemish-walnut writing-table, both from the 17th century, as well as a set of five typically Charles II-period walnut chairs. There are also two 17th-century Dutch chandeliers, which came from Deanery Garden, the house Lutyens designed for Hudson in Berkshire.

What was it like before?

Like the Dining Room, the vaulted ceiling here dates back to the late 18th century. However, prior to that, there wouldn't have been any rooms above and the gabled roof was designed to blow out in an explosion, so preserving the walls. The corridor from the entrance would have continued past each storeroom door to the left of the fireplace.

The Long Stairs
The Long Gallery

1. The Long Stairs

Lutyens' playful personality comes through in this first set of stairs inside the Castle. At the top is a peep-hole through which children (and possibly adults) could look out – despite there being a long drop below. Lutyens' wife, Emily, appears to have been less keen on such features. After visiting with the family in 1906, she became fearful that their son Robert would hurt himself at the Castle and never allowed him to visit Lindisfarne again.

Walking up the stairs today, the change in appearance tells a story. As part of the original building, the door at the top of the staircase would have been the only one in this area to lead directly on to the Upper Battery. This door also contains the oldest pieces of glass in the entire building. Leading to the Long Gallery is the first of three doorways in the Castle which possibly came from Lindisfarne Priory originally. The others are in the West Bedroom (see page 25).

2. The Long Gallery

In terms of architecture, the Long Gallery could well be the most important section of the Castle. It is one of the only completely new spaces Lutyens added, joining the two separate buildings of the old fort and providing sheltered access to the new North Bedrooms Lutyens built in 1912 (see page 24).

It occasionally doubled up as a bedroom; during the Lutyens' family visit in 1906, 'Nannie' and Ursula slept here, probably at the western end by the fireplace.

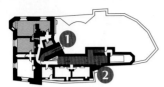

The Lutyens effect

Now one single arch marks the divide between Lutyens' architecture from the small room at the western end. The double arch on the central column was added along with a replacement staircase, newly covered, leading to the Upper Gallery at the western end.

This was where a fireplace was incorporated; the initials 'E H' and the date '1906' allude to this renovation period and the fireplace can be compared with that in the Entrance Hall, which also bears initials and a date.

What was once here?

Lutyens' Long Gallery links the former Commander's Lodgings on the Upper Battery with the old garrison barracks.

While home to the garrison, the area on the steps to the Long Gallery would have been open to the elements. So channels were cut into the

steps, leading to what was originally the Queen's Battery, which was added to the Castle between 1746 and 1819.

Sheltered from the prevailing westerly winds, the eastern rooms were used as officers' quarters. The words 'Artillery store for small stores' can still be seen on the green door leading to the Upper Battery.

Details and décor

The series of prints hanging on the walls in the Long Gallery were acquired by Hudson. They are by the German engraver Johannes Ridinger and are mostly of hunting scenes from the 18th century. There are titles in both German and French. Hudson was also responsible for the fire irons and hearth at the western end of the room.

Above Barbie Lutyens, one of Edwin Lutyens' children, playing a spinet in the Long Gallery, c.1906

Opposite Lutyens-designed archways in the Long Gallery

Left A close-up of Lutyens' herringbone floor pattern

The North and West Bedrooms

1. The North Bedrooms

This area was formerly occupied by the Queen's Battery, a north-facing gun battery installed between 1742 and 1813. It had to be prepared for any attacks coming from the north and had two levels.

This approach was previously unprotected; it's likely that the 1745 Jacobite rebellion brought this to the attention of the authorities.

The Lutyens effect

Added during Lutyens' second phase of renovation in 1912, the small bedrooms off the Long Gallery demonstrate how the designer had the ability to create the appearance and feel of a grand room in a fairly small space. Hudson then placed very large beds in the rooms which actually helped to make the spaces appear even bigger.

Two photographs provide 'before and after' views of the Long Gallery. A new doorway to the bedrooms is visible in the 'after' view, showing the Gallery pre-dates the bedrooms. These rooms were probably added to provide additional accommodation; Hudson previously had to borrow the island's manor house to lodge extra guests. Lutyens recalls his children sleeping in a Gun Room (this is possibly the room that is now the West Bedroom), and there not being enough beds because Hudson 'forgot to order them'.

Within this bulk of work was a third north bedroom, which looks over to the Walled Garden (see pages 32–35) and old parapet of the Queen's Battery (now covered with lead). This doesn't run parallel to the wall, so highlighting the curved shape of the former gun platform.

2. The West Bedroom

Dry, secure and a distance from the accommodation block in the east of the building, this was once a gunpowder store. When the light is just right, the word 'MAGAZINE' can still be seen on the door.

The Lutyens effect

Lutyens made little structural change here and kept original features such as the wooden beams at the far end of the room, which date back to the Castle's humble beginnings.

However he did add the dais (raised platform), brick floor and larger windows. In hindsight, considering the position of the room – high, with three external walls – and prevailing weather (the room faced into the wind), the latter might not have been the best idea, especially since this is the only bedroom without a fireplace.

Mostly thanks to Lutyens, the Castle is full of interesting doors. This room has another of the three medieval doorways possibly reused from Lindisfarne Priory. Of course Lutyens added his signature: an elegant door-handle. It also has its original lock, dating from around 1855.

The keyhole cover on the outside bears the motif 'W D' and the three-pointed 'broad arrow' of the government's War Department.

Lutyens was also responsible for the curved wall that guides visitors to the Upper Battery or back towards the Long Gallery.

'All his kind hospitality, yet he never thinks how people are going to get in.'

Lutyens, on Hudson's sleeping arrangements for guests

Opposite A view of the West Bedroom's bed

Left The West Bedroom today

Jekyll at Lindisfarne

The West Bedroom looks out over Lindisfarne's small Walled Garden. This was designed by the influential horticulturalist and garden designer Gertrude Jekyll (see pages 32–35). Accompanied by Lutyens, she visited the Castle in May 1906. They came over in a small boat, rowed to the island by Jack Lilburn, and Lutyens brought with him a raven called Black Jack, given to him by his dentist and kept in a Gladstone bag.

The pair arrived to rain and the Castle was, at this point, still very rugged. Despite this, Lutyens reported that Jekyll was 'quite charmed and so appreciative' and that during the musical evenings she sang along to the guitar. But as she was in her sixties, extremely short-sighted and rarely away from home, this was Jekyll's first and last visit to Lindisfarne.

The East Bedroom

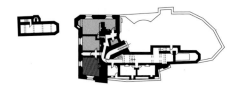

The largest and most sheltered of the Castle's nine bedrooms, this was probably where Hudson's most important guests stayed. Among them were leading choral conductor Sir Malcolm Sargent, the founder of the Scouting movement Lord Baden-Powell, and Lady Violet Bonham-Carter, a close friend of Churchill's, daughter of Asquith and grandmother to Helena.

However the long table features photographs of some of the Castle's more regular visitors: Barbie and Robert Lutyens. Hudson was very close to the Lutyens family, and even commissioned a series of photographs of the children at the Castle by *Country Life* photographer Charles Latham.

Their mother, Lady Emily, was less fond the Castle. During the family's ten-week holiday in October 1906 she highlighted a dislike for the cold, the way fires and candles smoked from the wind, and the dangers presented to her children.

The Lutyens effect

The route to this room is rather maze-like; something Lutyens no doubt had fun designing. It teases guests with twists and turns, including

Below A view of the East Bedroom

Opposite A dressing table in one of the North Bedrooms

steps down and up, all with the aim of creating the feeling that the Castle and space is much bigger than it actually is.

Lutyens continued this theme of playing with scale in the room itself. The imposing lintel above the tiny fireplace is one of his features.

He also had had various pieces designed specifically for this room: the three-pillared trestle table, which most likely would have been assembled in the room due to its size, as well as the pair of wall-cabinets.

The remaining furniture includes the bed, one of three in the Castle made in Flanders in 1753 – the other two are in one of the north bedrooms and the West Bedroom – and a William Morris settee that was most likely acquired either at auction or taken from one of Hudson's other properties.

The portraits

The picture above the fireplace is of Edwin Lutyens. It is from an unfinished Augustus John painting. Next to the door hangs a photograph of Edward Hudson. The National Trust probably installed these here in the 1980s.

What was once here?

Unlike many of the other bedrooms, the East Bedroom's dimensions have remained the same since the Castle was first built. Its use hasn't altered much either. An 1883 Board of Ordnance survey noted the eastern rooms as officers' quarters. With no evidence of an officer permanently serving at the Castle, the Master Gunner – or the person in charge of the detachment – would have had the pleasure of staying in this room.

Sheltered from westerly winds, it's likely the additional rooms in the eastern 'wing' of the Castle were used by the other gunners and their families since they would have been the most comfortable. Due to the lack of accommodation elsewhere in the Castle at the time, it's likely each room would have housed an entire family. These other rooms are now used as office space for National Trust staff and are not open to the public.

Keeping captives

Lindisfarne Castle was never intended as a prison, but in 1660 two men who had signed the death warrant of Charles I were held here before being transferred elsewhere. Robert Tichborne (left) and Henry Marten (right) were both tried as regicides; Tichborne was sentenced to death and Marten to internal exile.

The Upper Gallery

'I still remember all this lovely music that was for the visitors in the afternoon and in the evening she [Madame Suggia] played exclusively for islanders and all the fishermen,' recalled the Lilburns' family friend, Elfreda Elford, in 2004.

Elfreda was not the only person on Lindisfarne to be enchanted by Madame Suggia's performances. The renowned cellist was a frequent visitor to the Castle and often played for fellow guests after dinner, either here or in the Ship Room (see pages 20–21), perhaps using the 1717 Stradivarius cello Hudson gave her as a gift on their engagement in 1919. '[She] enchanted us by her immense vitality and charm,' said Siegfried Sassoon. 'Her cello's eloquence accompanied only by the beat and wash of waves breaking beneath the windows.' Suggia even held two concerts in aid of the village war memorial. The cello here today alludes to these concerts, though it is not the Stradivarius.

The Lutyens effect
Plans from an 1883 survey show that this room was being used for storage, and it is a fair assumption that this was always its purpose until Lutyens arrived.

At the western end he transformed the once-flat wall into an eye-pleasing bay shape, to include new windows that illuminate what would have been a very dark space. The dais at the opposite end was installed at Hudson's request, most likely to act as a stage for Madame Suggia's performances.

Access to the Upper Gallery was now provided via Lutyens' Long Gallery – something a little more suited to Hudson's guests since they couldn't very well be required to use an external door on the Upper Battery. Lutyens also designed the turret, which is accessed via the spiral stairway just outside the Upper Gallery (not open to the public).

'She was a striking woman with her scarves and flowing things. She was a lovely lady.'

Elfreda Elford

Below Madame Suggia performing in February 1925, photographed by Bertram Park

Opposite A view of the Upper Gallery

The furniture includes a Charles II chest-of-drawers inlaid with mother-of-pearl and ivory, a set of 19th-century spindle-back chairs and a Flemish marquetry fall-front bureau. At the platform end is an unusually shaped oak cupboard.

The engravings include 18th-century portraits, mainly of Italian artists, and a set depicting silk farming and weaving as it was carried out in one of the great Florentine houses of the 16th century. These were engraved by Philip Galle (1537–1612) after the originals by Jan Stradanus (1523–1605).

The Upper Battery

This area not only provides far-reaching views to the Farne Islands and towards Bamburgh Castle. You can also see exactly what Lutyens added to Lindisfarne.

Below Looking west from the Upper Battery, towards Holy Island, c.1913

Opposite A seal on Ross Sands, with Lindisfarne Castle in the distance

The Lutyens effect
One particularly clear feature is the Long Gallery: the enclosed carriage-like tunnel shows what would originally have been open space.

The Battery was re-surfaced during Lutyens' renovations; however, it largely retains its original form. Only a slight extension of the eastern building has decreased the overall area of the Upper Battery.

At the northern side, looking on to the Castle, Lutyens added the hexagonal turret. Notice the three chimneys (with precise gaps in-between) for the bedrooms.

On the western side and over towards the sea, between the original Long Stairs door and the building to the right, it appears as though there's almost a box in-between them. It originally would have been a gap, but that would have been too random for Lutyens.

To the right, there's almost a magic-eye staircase (no longer accessible today). It doesn't actually lead anywhere – another example of Lutyens' fun-loving behaviour.

Over the edge
As well as the garden (see pages 32–35), garden designer Gertrude Jekyll also planted up the crag on which the Castle stands. To access the difficult ledges, she enlisted seven-year-old islander Harry Walker. He was put in a pannier, and lowered to them from the Upper Battery.

How the Upper Battery evolved
The earliest mention of the Upper Battery dates to the early 17th century and records show there were as many as ten guns here, which would have been used for protection. Armament grew due to threats from the Dutch (with whom Britain was at war) and Flemish pirates.

'The moon is up and a long beam of light stretching across the sea from Bamburgh Castle on the mainland. Curlews are calling, and always the waves are lapping on the rocks. There is a smell of seaweed.'
Oswald Falk, 1930

Top Tip
Sometimes volunteers man the Battery with binoculars and telescopes – ask to borrow these to see a close-up of seals along the coast.

While it is the larger battery, this area only had to cover the channel and the harbour, not the coastal approaches as the better-armed Lower Battery did. An emplacement for a rifled 64-pounder muzzle-loading gun was installed to replace the older fixed guns in 1882, as part of the Castle's last armament, but it was removed in 1893.

Claim to fame
In 1965, Roman Polanski's tense classic *Cul-de-Sac* was shot in and around the Castle. The film starred Donald Pleasance, Françoise Dorléac, and Lionel Stander and is widely regarded as one of Polanski's finest pieces of work. It also provides excellent records of the building in the 1960s.

Gertrude's glorious garden

Above This illustration of Jekyll can be seen on the inside of the Walled Garden

Right Gertrude Jekyll, possibly in her Munstead Wood garden

When it came to finding a designer for the Walled Garden it was only natural for Lutyens to contact his trusted friend and fellow Arts and Crafts practitioner Gertrude Jekyll.

Jekyll (1843–1932) was already an accomplished garden designer when she first met Edwin Lutyens at Littleworth Cross, Surrey, in May 1889. Their encounter heralded the start of a collaborative partnership that lasted until Jekyll's death.

Around this time, Jekyll was a new contributor to *Country Life* magazine and became friends with the editor, Edward Hudson. It's conceivable that Jekyll first introduced Hudson and Lutyens. Jekyll worked with Lutyens on Hudson's Berkshire home, Deanery Garden in Sonning, Berkshire, and had him design her own home in Surrey, Munstead Wood.

Jekyll's career
'Bumps' – as Lutyens affectionately called her – enrolled in South Kensington School of Art, London in 1861, six years after Lutyens. Here she studied botany, optics, anatomy and the science of colour.

Jekyll designed her first garden in 1860: her mother's at Munstead House, just across the road from the Lutyens-designed house Jekyll would later live in. The design was well received by experts and marked the beginning of a career that included creating over 400 gardens, writing more than 1,000 magazine articles, and authoring 13 books. Jekyll also ran a garden centre in Godalming, Surrey, where she bred many new plants, something she continued well into her eighties at Munstead Wood.

Jekyll worked on the principle put forward by William Robinson in 1870, that there should be more freedom in garden planting than there had been in traditional Victorian gardens. She was also one of the first garden designers to take into account colour and texture in her plans. So she was the perfect choice to take on the Walled Garden at Lindisfarne Castle.

Left Lindisfarne's garden in August. In the foreground are the yellow crown daisy (*Chrysanthemum coronarium*) and cornflowers (*Centaurea cyanus*). 'Purple Emperor' (*Sedum telephium*) can be seen in the central bed

Designing Lindisfarne

We think the Castle sits within a designed landscape, with the garden's position planned as part of that. Originally Jeykll considered planting near the Castle, but those plans were quickly redirected to a more suitable area. The existing small, enclosed kitchen garden – which would have served the garrison in previous years – became the chosen plot. Its high ground, existing wall and the fact that it had been previously cultivated made it an appealing back-up option.

However Hudson's ambitious plans for a walled croquet lawn, tennis court and two gatehouses had to be jettisoned. They possibly fell foul of the greater expense of flooding the field to create a lake, which depleted funds.

To ensure that guests had the best view of the Castle, the garden's entrance was moved from the north wall to the south. The outward-facing wall was then lowered to provide a scenic backdrop, with Beblowe Crag taking centre stage.

'A garden is a grand teacher. It teaches patience and careful watchfulness; it teaches industry and thrift; above all it teaches entire trust.'

Gertrude Jekyll

Lutyens' plan included a formal pattern of flower-beds and stone paths defying the irregular geometry. When looking at the garden from the Castle, the walls and the paved walks are designed to give the illusion of a greater size – typical of his work.

Meanwhile, Jekyll devised a planting scheme for the one-eighth-of-an-acre space. She worked in conjunction with Lutyens, who designed the alterations to the garden wall and pathways within. The planting plan for the garden was prepared in 1911 so, as Jekyll only visited the island once in 1906 (see page 25), she was not present for the actual planting.

The Jekyll effect

Jekyll's garden was designed to be at its best from July to September, when Hudson was most commonly in residence; this remains the case today.

'I can sow mint, thyme, sage, sorrel, chives, savory.'

Gertrude Jekyll, writing in her notebook

The designer first considered a vegetable garden encompassing sweet peas, most likely for their pleasant smell and colours that would attract fertilising insects, as well as other annuals. However, it was soon re-thought, to concentrate on specific flowers, including both annuals and perennials, as well as plants that worked well as cut flowers, presumably to be used inside the Castle itself.

Jekyll cleverly made use of silvery grey foliage to echo the stone and draw in the light, such as edgings of standard and silver-carpeted lamb's ear (*Stachys byzantina*).

Flowers included eight varieties of sweet peas, including the delicate 'Elizabeth Taylor' and the deep crimson 'Queen Alexandra'. These encompass either side of the main axis, almost providing a frame to the Castle, as well as screening off the vegetables.

Splashes of bright colour, especially during July and August, are provided by the side borders where the dark red shrub rose 'Hugh Dickson' and the rare 1898 'Killarney' rose flower along with another Jekyll favourite, 'Zéphirine Drouhin'. There's also purple Jackman's clematis (*Clematis* u jackmanii), lavenders and sweet-scented mignonette.

The south-facing border blends the more vibrant reds and burgundy of tall hollyhocks, bergamot and fuchsias with the yellows and whites of sunflowers (*Helianthus annuus* 'Pastiche'), cotton lavender (*Santolina*) and Japanese anemones.

Shoots from Jekyll's own 'Munstead Red' sedum sit in the central bed, surrounded by the Caucasian scabious, *Scabiosa caucasica* 'Clive Greaves', cornflowers and delphiniums.

In September, an abundance of 'silver cup' tree mallows (*Lavatera trimestris*) and chrysanthemums adorn the pathways. The centres of the globe artichokes display purple flowers.

Then there's the little touches of Jekyll's genius, such as using the spent stems of the delphiniums as supports for the angelic virgin's bower (*Clematis flammula*).

The future is bright

In 2003 a large project took place: the replanting of the Walled Garden. Research and archaeology was carried out by Michael Tooley of Durham University, his wife Rosanna and a group of volunteer students.

Although the team followed Jekyll's 1911 plan and planting schemes as closely as possible, some of the species she had planted no longer exist, so closely matched alternatives were used.

Right An abundance of plants, including yellow chrysanthemums and orange calendulas, in Lindisfarne's Jekyll-designed garden

An industrial heritage: Lindisfarne's Lime Kilns

The Lime Kilns at Castle Point on Holy Island are among the largest, most complex and best preserved in Northumberland.

The Kilns are a Scheduled Ancient Monument, in recognition of the national significance of the site. They are one of the largest examples of their kind anywhere in the country and certainly the largest actively conserved kilns in the area.

They also offer a window to the island's industrial past. For hundreds of years, limestone was roasted on Holy Island, producing quick lime for a variety of uses such as agricultural fertiliser, mortar for buildings and whitewash.

Castle Point houses six lime kilns arranged in a rectangular formation (25m x 30m). Within it are six pots and a network of access tunnels. The three nearest the Castle have four draw arches and the three farthest away have three arches, where the roasted lime was removed.

From cart to kiln

Lime was quarried on the north of the island, then transported to the southern shore for export (there was no deep water anchorage closer to the quarry itself). Holy Island offered the perfect position for a limestone quarry as its proximity to the sea allowed for easy exportation to Scotland. By the 19th century, quick lime was being produced on an industrial scale.

Businessman William Nicoll happened to own a fleet of ships, which brought coal from Scotland to the staithes (wooden jetties) and took the quick lime away. Six ships sailed regularly during the 1860s.

Horses dragged tubs filled with stone from the north of the island and coal from the ships to the Kilns. Once there, workers would push the cart to the top of the pots to spare the horse having to suffer the unimaginable heat. The finished quick lime was then taken back to the staithes for export.

The end of the industry

In the 1860s, one in five island men worked in the lime industry, but by the 1880s only one man was working at the Kilns, with four employed at the quarry. The industry was in decline.

The last record of Nicoll's ships leaving Holy Island with a cargo of lime was on 17 September 1883. While Nicoll still relied on the sea for transport, the lime industry on the mainland was increasingly making use of the coastal railways.

It is thought these Kilns were last fired by a farmer in around 1900. Today, the remains of the two staithes and several of the iron mooring rings where the ships would have been tied up can still be seen on the foreshore, near the Castle gate.

Left The Lime Kilns, with Lindisfarne Castle in the distance

Right The old wooden staithes that once served the Lime Kilns can still be seen at Lindisfarne

Saints and Soldiers: Lindisfarne's Earlier History

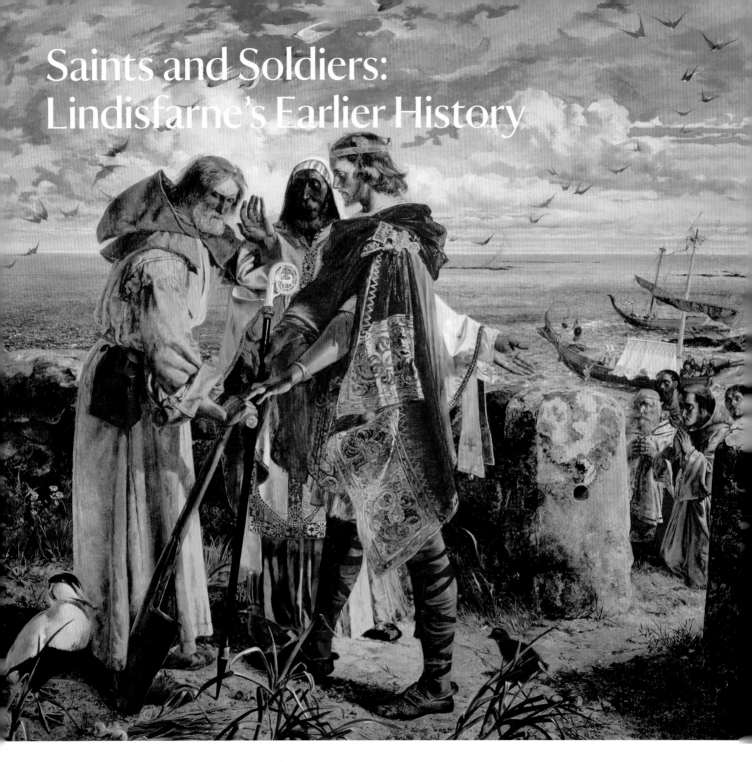

It could be said that the first inhabitants of Lindisfarne Castle arrived more through necessity than choice.

When St Aidan was ordered to found a monastic community on this remote spot in AD635, he decided that the more sheltered ground on the south-west corner of the island, away from the North Sea gales, would be the best site.

St Aidan was succeeded by Cuthbert and their lifelong work – along with the discovery of St Aidan's miraculously preserved body – created quite a stir and inspired the Lindisfarne Gospels. This put Lindisfarne on the map and made it a designated place of pilgrimage.

With this came wealth, and with that came greed. The monks had become a target. However, with the vista high up from Beblowe Crag, a geological formation of almost mythical appearance, the monks were able to watch for any threat coming their way – especially the Danish Vikings and Scots pillaging the coastlands.

In 793 the church itself was gutted by 'the heathen' and the last Danish raid in 875 drove out the monks, who took the precious relics of St Aidan, St Cuthbert and the Lindisfarne Gospels on a seven-year journey.

Some Benedictine monks from Durham Cathedral, where St Cuthbert's relics had come to rest, returned to the island in 1082. Fifty years on, they re-established The Priory Church and christened Lindisfarne 'Holy Island' in Cuthbert's memory.

The Scottish wars

For the next 500 years, Lindisfarne was rarely affected by the warfare on the mainland. But then, in 1537, Henry VIII dissolved Lindisfarne Priory and the other medieval monasteries.

This brought Holy Island to the forefront of his conflict with Scotland in a way it hadn't been in the past, and for the first time the priory buildings and harbour were used for warfare.

The Scots were on a rampage, continuing their devastation of the border counties as well as cementing a new alliance with the French. Holy Island's harbour proved invaluable in fighting them. In 1544, during his punitive expedition against the Scots, Edward Seymour, Lord Hertford landed over 2,000 troops on his way to attack Edinburgh and ten English warships anchored in the haven.

Protecting the island

In 1542, a couple of years before Lord Hertford's expedition, Lindisfarne's fortification was planned. Two bulwarks (defensive walls) were ordered – one to command the road and the other to defend the island.

And so in 1549 an artillery fort was constructed using stone quarried from the Priory which had been closed since its dissolution. The building was first constructed as a simple gun platform to defend the harbour. In the 1560s, this was replaced by a fort.

Left King Egfrid and Bishop Trumwine landing on the Farne Islands to persuade Cuthbert to be made Bishop. Dating from 1856, this is one of a series of eight oil paintings by William Bell Scott, which together illustrate the history of the English border. It is currently on display at Wallington, Northumberland (also National Trust)

'The forte of Beblowe, within the Holy Island, lyeth very well for the defence of the haven there. The Holy Island is a place much necessarye to be defended and preserved, for there is a harboroughe sufficient for a great navye of ships to rest safely in, and very aptlye for the wars towards Scotland. And in that Island be both store houses, brewe houses, and backe houses, to conserve and prepare victualls sufficient to furnish the said navye withall; which store houses must either contynuallye be kept in reparations, or ells they will shortlye decaye.'

Sir Robert Bowes, March Warden, in a 1550 survey

The 16th to 19th centuries

In 1570, aware of an imminent threat from the north, Queen Elizabeth dispatched engineers to 'fix' the Castle's dilapidated gun platform. The work was carried out over the course of two years. The new and improved fort was defended by the best, but it would be some years before it was tested.

When James I took the crown, England and Scotland were united, and so Lindisfarne Castle lost much of its strategic importance. However it was still used by the garrison, which in 1559 consisted of a captain, two master gunners (on one shilling per day), one master's mate (on ten pennies per day) and twenty soldiers (on eight pennies per day).

Capturing the Castle

Following the capture of Berwick in May 1643, the parliamentarian garrison there sent a warship to persuade the men in the fort to side with them. After negotiations failed, action was taken: a parliamentarian chronicle of 1644 noted that 'we let fly a broadside at it, and they answered again in our own language; the cannons thus playing awhile on both sides, and yet no hurt done'.

This is the first (and only) instance of the Castle being attacked and firing its cannon in anger. In order to end the affair though, the Captain of the warship decided on 'running our ships under the Castle, and landing one hundred men, they came to parley, and yielded, upon conditions to have them a year's pay … and so [we] became masters of that impregnable castle of Holy Island'. The Castle surrendered on 1 June 1643.

'The Castle is our own!'

By 1715, the garrison on Holy Island consisted of just seven men. That year, drama knocked at the door when Lancelot Errington, the master of a brigantine at anchor in the harbour, paid a visit to the Master Gunner – who was also an amateur barber – apparently to be shaved. Errington returned a little later with his nephew, Mark, claiming to have lost his watch. They threatened the Master Gunner with pistols, and crying 'Damn you, the Castle is our own!', ejected him and the only other soldier on duty.

They raised The Old Pretender's flag and enjoyed a taste of Jacobite glory – for one night only. They fired the guns on the Lower Battery as a signal to the French fleet they thought was coming to support them, but the fleet didn't actually arrive until two days later. In the meantime, the fort was swiftly re-captured by some soldiers from Berwick. The men were arrested and taken to Berwick gaol, but they burrowed their way out. After spending nine days hidden in a pea stack near Bamburgh Castle, they escaped.

Opposite *Lindisfarne Castle and Abbey, Holy Island, by Moonlight*, an oil painting on canvas by John Moore, 1877

The end of the Fort

The Castle remained in the Crown's hands and was garrisoned, at least in times of stress, by a small detachment from Berwick. The old muzzles were later removed to make way for 156 barrels of gunpowder and three 64-pounders – the Castle's last and grandest armament.

When the Castle garrison was disbanded in 1819, the fort was used as a coastguard station.

From 1878, it became a coastal artillery drill station for a detachment of the Royal Artillery Volunteers, who finally withdrew some 15 years later.

From then until Hudson came along, the Castle was left uninhabited but used periodically by coastguards. In the meantime, Holy Island prospered due to profits from limestone quarrying, herring fishing, farming and tourism.

Wildlife

Holy Island offers pockets of heavenly habitats for wildlife.

It is because of the surrounding land and soils that rare plants grow here, providing coastal commuters with delicacies to eat and an ideal breeding season. It's also one of the largest intertidal areas in the North East of England and was designated a Site of Special Scientific Interest in 1981, as part of the wider Lindisfarne National Nature Reserve managed by Natural England.

Grasslands

Dwarf eelgrass is one of a very few flowering plants that live in seawater, creating underwater meadows that are perfect for marine wildlife to feast on. It also creates a safe haven for species of flatfish to lay their eggs and shelter their newborns. The roots of eelgrass bind the sand, helping to naturally preserve and prevent erosion of the seabed.

Butterflies and moths

Don't be surprised to see wonderful dashes of colour fluttering by during the summer months.

In June to early September, look out for dark fritillaries, who love chalk and limestone grassland. Grayling butterflies are a little harder to spot as their underwings ensure they're well camouflaged – perhaps that is why they rest with closed wings. When opened, expect flashes of pale orange and yellow bands.

Mesmerising ringlets, almost velvety in appearance, have wings fringed with white and small circles on their underwings. They enjoy feasting on brambles.

Rare moths visit too. *Aphelia unitana* can be seen and gorgeous *Crambus uliginosellus* enjoy wet boggy grasslands. Both tend to make an appearance from June to July.

Seals

Beblowe Crag is an ideal vantage point to see wildlife, including grey seals who spend their time out at sea feeding on fish, but love the rocky shores and sand dunes along the coastline. The more common seals, or harbour seals, prefer sheltered shores to haul out on the sandbanks and beaches. Smaller than grey seals, their colours can vary but they generally sport dark spots, just like the greys.

Rock pool regulars

August to October is a great time to examine rock pools at the coast. Each will have a life of its own – a bustling village for a variety of seaweeds, crabs, tiny fish, limpets and other wonderful creatures.

Left A young female grey seal

This page Grasses on the north of Holy Island

Lindisfarne's birds

A number of feathered creatures might be spotted during a trip to Lindisfarne.

1. Swallows These agile pilots spend most of their time in the air. They have dark, glossy blue backs, red chins and pale underbodies, and can be seen in the Lime Kilns, where it's relatively quiet with plenty of tunnels to glide through. They also sometimes nest in the Castle.

2. Fulmars These coastal birds are often mistaken for gulls, but they're actually related to the albatross. They fly low over the sea, gliding and banking. To approach their breeding site, they ride the up-draught high up the cliff face, protecting their nest from intruders by spitting out foul-smelling oil. You may also spot them sitting on the spout just below the wall of the Upper Battery.

3. Rock pipits Streaked olive-brown and off-white underneath, these large and stocky birds can often be seen on the Castle's gun batteries and the rocks below. They also love rocky beaches (most likely for the small fish and shellfish) so the coast is the perfect place for them to breed.

4. Geese The largest and bulkiest of the wild geese, greylags can be seen from September to March.

Brent geese, the light-bellied ones, fly in loose flocks right along the coast, visiting from October through to March, nibbling away at the eelgrass.

5. Gannets Bright white with black wingtips, gannets have long necks and long, pointed beaks, tails and wings. They tend to hunt for fish by first gliding low over water, then flying high and circling, before plunging into the sea. You might spot them doing this from Castle Point.

Cormorants Cormorants are fairly large, black and almost goose-like. Spot them gliding between roosts or perhaps perched on the rocks in the sea, between the Castle and Ross Sands.

Ducks Four species of duck can be spotted at Lindisfarne.

Eider ducks are the most commonly seen at the Castle; they're also known as 'Cuddy' ducks, after St Cuthbert (see pages 38–39).

Common scoters are a small, diving sea-duck, often spotted out at sea in a crowd, like large bobbing rafts. They arrive in large numbers around October and stay until March. They breed elsewhere from June to July. However, their breeding has declined and the common scoter is now a Red List (globally threatened) species.

Wigeons can be seen all-year-round, eating plants and grasses. Males have chestnut heads and necks with yellow foreheads, while females are all brown.

Very colourful and fairly big, shelducks are extremely pretty, with distinctive markings and dark green heads and necks.

Terns Artic terns from the Farnes, as well as common and sandwich terns, can often be heard – if not always seen – from the Castle. A small colony is cared for on the rocks in the middle of the channel leading to the harbour.

Whooper swans Making their way here from October to March, whooper swans are bigger than Bewick's swans. They can often be seen near the Holy Island causeway. They have long, thin necks and black bills that each sport a large yellow triangle.

Preserving History

With the help of donors, members and invaluable support from the local village, various processes have been undertaken to conserve Lindisfarne Castle.

One of the building's most endearing qualities is also one of the factors that quietly impacts it the most. Both wind and rain take their toll on the exterior and interior of the Castle. It's one of the National Trust's biggest concerns.

Swirly lines on the external stones at the Upper Battery ironically look decorative – they are actually caused by constant exposure to the ferocious coastal weather.

Lutyens' bigger windows allow in so much natural light that it has an adverse effect upon the objects inside. So black-out curtains are also hung throughout winter. They are drawn back only minutes before the doors are opened to the public. There's even a light monitor that

transmits data to a central recording unit to enable the levels to be constantly monitored. Most windows are covered with UV filters.

Heavy rain tends to seep in through the windows too. Unfortunately, it doesn't only affect the windows but the wooden panes, the plaster on the walls and the floor below.

Housekeeping

The Wind Indicator in the Entrance Hall (see pages 14–15) is extremely intricate and in April 2006 its first major conservation project was carried out. It was the first time it had been taken apart since 1913. It's in good working order, and still tells the wind direction today.

In the Kitchen, a layer of late 20th-century paint was removed from the back of the range in 2008, revealing the original white tiles.

The portcullis Lutyens installed still works, and is lowered and raised twice a year to ensure that it stays that way.

Carpets in the Castle are usually sacrificial, protecting floors such as Lutyens' beautifully placed herringbone patterns from high footfall. They can be replaced, usually every ten years, depending on various factors.

Outdoors, the team continues to survey the wildlife, as well as improving access to certain areas, while working to a conservation management plan.

The National Trust wouldn't be unable to continue preserving a special place like this without a trusty team of volunteers helping behind the scenes.

Thank you, everyone, for your support.

Opposite Major conservation work on the Wind Indicator in progress, 2006

Left above The north wall being covered with a render, or 'harling', which needs to be regularly checked and maintained

Left below Cementitious mortars are removed and replaced with porous lime-based pointing

The View from the Upper Battery

Longstone Lighthouse

Bamburgh Castle

The Farne Islands

Castle Point Lime Kilns